For the One who created hummingbirds.

—*Genesis* 1:20

Published by
PEACHTREE PUBLISHERS
1700 Chattahoochee Avenue
Atlanta, Georgia 30318-2112
www.peachtree-online.com

Text © 2011 by Cathryn P. Sill
Illustrations © 2011 by John C. Sill

First trade paperback edition published in 2015

Illustrations created in watercolor on archival quality 100% rag watercolor paper
Text and titles set in Novarese from Adobe Systems

Printed in June 2017 by Imago in Singapore
10 9 8 7 6 5 4 3 2 (hardcover)
10 9 8 7 6 5 4 3 2 (trade paperback)

Library of Congress Cataloging-in-Publication Data

Sill, Cathryn P., 1953-
　About hummingbirds / written by Cathryn Sill ; illustrated by John Sill.
　　p. cm.
　ISBN 978-1-56145-588-1 (hardcover) / 978-1-56145-837-0 (trade paperback)
　1. Hummingbirds—Juvenile literature. I. Sill, John, ill. II. Title.
　QL696.A558S54 2011
　598.7'64—dc22
　　　　　　　　　　2010051999

About Hummingbirds

A Guide for Children

Cathryn Sill

Illustrated by John Sill

PEACHTREE

ATLANTA

Hummingbirds are small birds
that get food from flowers.

They have sharp narrow bills and long tongues
that help them reach into blossoms for nectar.

a.

e.

b.

d.

c.

Hummingbirds also hunt and eat small insects and spiders.

They often fight over food.

Hummingbirds are the only birds that fly forward, backward, sideways, and even upside down.

They can easily hover in one place.

Most hummingbirds cannot walk.
Their feet are used for perching.

All hummingbirds are small. Many are tiny.

Most male hummingbirds have bright
shiny feathers that seem to change colors
in different lights.

Female hummingbirds usually have duller colored feathers. This helps them hide as they sit on their nests.

Mother hummingbirds build nests from materials such as twigs, leaves, down from plants, moss, lichens, and spiderwebs.

Each lays two small white eggs and raises the chicks with no help from the father.

Larger animals sometimes hunt for hummingbird nests and eat the eggs or chicks.

Adult hummingbirds are usually fast enough to escape from predators.

Hummingbirds live in different habitats.

Some hummingbirds live in one area
all year long.

Others migrate long distances as the seasons change.

It is important to protect hummingbirds and the places where they live.

PLATE 18
Black-breasted Puffleg

Afterword

PLATE 1
There are more than 325 species of hummingbirds in the world. Hummingbirds are found only in the Americas. Most hummingbirds live in the tropics. Ruby-throated Hummingbirds spend the winter in Mexico, in Central America, and on Caribbean islands. They migrate across the Gulf of Mexico to North America in spring. Ruby-throats are the only hummingbirds that nest in eastern North America.

PLATE 2
Hummingbirds have special forked tongues with fringed edges that help them lap nectar from flowers. The size and shape of hummingbird bills often match the flowers they feed on. Sword-billed Hummingbirds have the longest bills—up to 4 ½ inches (11.4 cm) long. They find food in large flowers in the Andes Mountains of South America. Purple-backed Thornbills have the shortest bills and feed from smaller flowers in the Andes. Buff-tailed Sicklebills live in the eastern Andes. Violet-crowned Hummingbirds are found in the southwestern United States and Mexico. Berylline Hummingbirds live in Mexico and Central America.

PLATE 3
Hummingbirds have two ways of hunting insects and spiders. They may swoop down to catch flying insects, using a method called "hawking." Sometimes they gather insects and spiders from plants or spiderwebs. Booted Racquet-tails are common in the cloud forests of South America, from Columbia to Peru.

PLATE 4

Hummingbirds need to eat large amounts because they burn so much energy. Most of them defend their food sources by chasing other birds away. Two hummingbirds sometimes lock their bills as they fight in the air. This can cause them to fall to the ground. Velvet-purple Coronets live in wet mossy forests and forest borders on the western slope of the Andes Mountains in southwestern Colombia and northwestern Ecuador.

PLATE 5

Some hummingbirds beat their wings as fast as 80 times per second. They are able to hold their wings in many different positions. Unlike other birds, hummingbirds cannot fold their wings. The ability to flap their stiff wings up and down rapidly makes hummingbirds powerful fliers. Broad-billed Hummingbirds are native to the southwestern United States and central and western Mexico.

PLATE 6

Hummingbirds are the only birds that can hover for long periods of time. They vigorously flap their wings forward and backward to stay in one place. Hummingbirds have to be strong since hovering uses a lot of energy. Frilled Coquettes live in the edges of forests in the lowlands of Brazil. They are often found on coffee plantations and around flower gardens.

PLATE 7

Most hummingbirds have small feet that are not strong enough for walking. They use their feet to perch for long periods of time while resting or while preening their feathers. Hummingbirds do not push with their feet when they leave the perch. They take off by flapping their wings and flying. Horned Sungems have feathers above and behind their eyes that look like horns. They live mainly in Brazil and Bolivia.

PLATE 8

The smallest birds in the world are the Bee Hummingbirds. They are about 2 inches (5 cm) long. Bee Hummingbirds live in Cuba. Giant Hummingbirds are the largest hummingbirds. They are around 8 inches (20–22 cm) long. Giant Hummingbirds live in the Andes Mountains of South America. Their larger size helps them keep warm in the cooler mountain temperatures. Female hummingbirds are usually bigger than males. Being larger makes it easier for them to lay eggs and take care of their babies.

PLATE 9

Hummingbird feathers are iridescent. The colors seem to change as the birds move. The feathers appear to glitter and shimmer in the light. Seen in indirect lighting or from other angles, their feathers look dull and black. Magnificent Hummingbirds are one of the two largest types of hummingbirds north of Mexico. They are around 5 inches (12 cm) long. Magnificent Hummingbirds live in the southwestern United States, Mexico, and Central America.

PLATE 10

The duller colors of female hummingbirds provide camouflage among the leaves and twigs and help them hide from enemies. Most young male hummingbirds are protectively camouflaged like the females for the first few months of their lives. Blue-throated Hummingbirds get their name from the patch of blue feathers on the throat of the male. The female has a plain gray throat. Blue-throated Hummingbirds live in the southwestern United States and Mexico.

PLATE 11

Hummingbirds usually build nests in places that offer protection from direct sun and rain. Many hummingbirds cover the outside of their nests with plant parts, moss, or lichen to make it harder for predators to find them. They hold their nests together with spiderwebs and line them with soft materials such as plant down, animal fur, or feathers. Buff-bellied Hummingbirds build cup-shaped nests on small branches or forked twigs. They live in southern Texas (USA), eastern Mexico, and parts of Central America.

PLATE 12

Hummingbird eggs usually take from fifteen to twenty-two days to hatch. Mother hummingbirds spend most of their time keeping the eggs and newly hatched chicks warm. The adult females only leave the nest to find food. Even after the young birds leave the nest, their mothers continue to feed them for several days. Anna's Hummingbirds are the only hummingbirds that regularly spend the winter in the United States. They live along the west coast of North America from southwestern Canada to northwestern Mexico.

PLATE 13
Hummingbird eggs and chicks are in danger from nest-robbers such as larger birds, reptiles, and squirrels. To defend their nests and guard their babies, mother hummingbirds will attack predators much larger than themselves. Female Broad-tailed Hummingbirds often return to the same nest site year after year. Broad-tails live in the western United States in summer. They migrate to Mexico and Guatemala in winter.

PLATE 14
Animals that hunt hummingbirds include snakes, hawks, domestic cats, praying mantises, and large spiders. Eyelash Pit Vipers sometimes wait at flowers on trees until hummingbirds appear. They strike as the birds feed. Rufous-tailed Hummingbirds live in central-eastern Mexico, Central America, and northwestern South America.

PLATE 15
Hummingbird habitats need to provide food, water, resting perches, and shelter from weather and predators. Hummingbirds live in places as far north as Alaska and as far south as Chile. Costa's Hummingbirds live in deserts in the southwestern United States and western Mexico. Calliope Hummingbirds are the smallest birds in North America. They spend the summer in mountains in western North America and migrate to southwestern and south-central Mexico in winter. White-tailed Goldenthroats often live in wet grasslands in parts of South America. Crimson Topazes are native to the rainforests of northern South America.

PLATE 16

Hummingbirds that live in the tropics are able to find food all year without having to travel long distances. They may move up and down mountains as the seasons change. Great Sapphirewings are one of the largest humming-birds. They are about 7½ inches (19–20 cm) long. Great Sapphirewings live in the Andes Mountains of Columbia, Ecuador, Bolivia, and Peru.

PLATE 17

Most of the hummingbirds found in North America migrate north in spring. In fall when flowers stop blooming, they migrate south to spend the winter in places where they can find food. Rufous Hummingbirds migrate farther north than any other kind of hummingbird—as far as parts of Alaska. They spend summers in western North America and winters in Mexico and along the Gulf Coast of the United States.

PLATE 18

Many flowers depend on hummingbirds for pollination. The pollen sticks to their heads and bills and the birds carry it from flower to flower. Without pollination, flowers cannot make seeds and reproduce. Several humming-bird species are threatened because of habitat destruction. Black-breasted Pufflegs are critically endangered. The places where they live are being cleared for ranchland, farmland, and charcoal production. The remaining Black-breasted Pufflegs are found only in one small area of Ecuador.

GLOSSARY

Camouflage—colors or patterns on an animal that help it hide
Habitat—the place where animals and plants live
Iridescent—having colors that seem to change when seen from different angles
Nectar—the sweet liquid formed in flowers
Perch—a place where a bird can sit and rest
Pollination—the transfer of pollen that causes seeds to form
Predator—an animal that hunts and eats other animals
Preening—the act of straightening and cleaning feathers with bills and feet
Species—a group of animals or plants that are alike in many ways
Tropical—having to do with the area around the equator

SUGGESTIONS FOR FURTHER READING

BOOKS

HUMMINGBIRDS: A BEGINNER'S GUIDE by Laurel Aziz (Firefly Books)
HUMMINGBIRDS by Mark J. Rauzon (Children's Press)
ZOOBOOKS: HUMMINGBIRDS by Timothy Biel (Wildlife Education, Ltd.)

WEBSITES

http://ibc.lynxeds.com/family/hummingbirds-trochilidae
http://www.birdwatching-bliss.com/hummingbirds.html
http://www.sandiegozoo.org/animalbytes/t-hummingbird.html

RESOURCES ESPECIALLY HELPFUL IN DEVELOPING THIS BOOK

HANDBOOK OF THE BIRDS OF THE WORLD: VOL. 5, Edited by Josep del Hoyo,
    Andrew Elliott, Jordi Sargatal (Lynx Edicions, Barcelona)
HUMMINGBIRDS: THEIR LIFE AND BEHAVIOR by Esther and Robert Tyrrell
    (Crown Publishers, Inc., New York)
HUMMINGBIRDS by Scott Weidensaul (Portland House, The Image Bank)

ABOUT... SERIES

ISBN 978-1-56145-234-7 HC
ISBN 978-1-56145-312-2 PB

ISBN 978-1-56145-038-1 HC
ISBN 978-1-56145-364-1 PB

ISBN 978-1-56145-688-8 HC
ISBN 978-1-56145-699-4 PB

ISBN 978-1-56145-301-6 HC
ISBN 978-1-56145-405-1 PB

ISBN 978-1-56145-256-9 HC
ISBN 978-1-56145-335-1 PB

ISBN 978-1-56145-588-1 HC

ISBN 978-1-56145-207-1 HC
ISBN 978-1-56145-232-3 PB

ISBN 978-1-56145-757-1 HC
ISBN 978-1-56145-758-8 PB

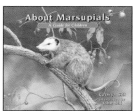

ISBN 978-1-56145-358-0 HC
ISBN 978-1-56145-407-5 PB

ISBN 978-1-56145-331-3 HC
ISBN 978-1-56145-406-8 PB

ISBN 978-1-56145-795-3 HC

ISBN 978-1-56145-743-4 HC
ISBN 978-1-56145-741-0 PB

ISBN 978-1-56145-536-2 HC
ISBN 978-1-56145-811-0 PB

ISBN 978-1-56145-183-8 HC
ISBN 978-1-56145-233-0 PB

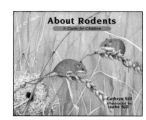

ISBN 978-1-56145-454-9 HC

ALSO AVAILABLE
IN BILINGUAL EDITION

- About Birds / Sobre los pájaros
  ISBN 978-1-56145-783-0 PB
- About Mammals / Sobre los mamíferos
  ISBN 978-1-56145-800-4 PB

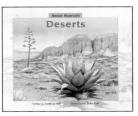

ISBN 978-1-56145-641-3 HC
ISBN 978-1-56145-636-9 PB

ISBN 978-1-56145-734-2 HC

ISBN 978-1-56145-559-1 HC

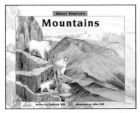

ISBN 978-1-56145-469-3 HC
ISBN 978-1-56145-731-1 PB

ISBN 978-1-56145-618-5 HC

ISBN 978-1-56145-432-7 HC
ISBN 978-1-56145-689-5 PB

THE SILLS

Cathryn Sill, a former elementary school teacher, is the author of the acclaimed ABOUT… series and ABOUT HABITATS series. With her husband John and her brother-in-law Ben Sill, she coauthored the popular bird-guide parodies, A FIELD GUIDE TO LITTLE-KNOWN AND SELDOM-SEEN BIRDS OF NORTH AMERICA, ANOTHER FIELD GUIDE TO LITTLE-KNOWN AND SELDOM-SEEN BIRDS OF NORTH AMERICA, and BEYOND BIRDWATCHING.

John Sill is a prize-winning and widely published wildlife artist who illustrated the ABOUT… series and ABOUT HABITATS series, and illustrated and coauthored the FIELD GUIDES and BEYOND BIRDWATCHING. A native of North Carolina, he holds a B.S. in Wildlife Biology from North Carolina State University.

The Sills live in Franklin, North Carolina.